An Exaltation of Starlings

Tom Conaty

𝔑 DOGHOUSE

An Exaltation of Starlings

is published by
DOGHOUSE
P.O. Box 312
Tralee G.P.O.
Co. Kerry
Ireland
TEL: +353 (0)66 7137547
www.doghousebooks.ie
email: doghouse312@eircom.net

© Tom Conaty, April 2010

ISBN 978-0-9558746-8-0

Edited for DOGHOUSE by Noel King

Cover illustration: Untitled, Struan Hamilton
www.struanhamilton.com

The publisher and poet thank
Cavan County Council
for its grant for this volume.

Further copies available at €12, postage free, from the above address,
cheques etc. payable to DOGHOUSE also PAYPAL - www.paypal.com to
doghousepaypal@eircom.net

Doghouse is a non-profit taking company, aiming to publish the best of literary
works by Irish born writers. Donations are welcome and will be acknowledged on
this page.

For our 2010 publications, many thanks to
Kerry Education Service.

KERRY
EDUCATION
SERVICE
Seirbhís Oideachais Chiarraí

Printed by Tralee Printing Works, Monavalley Industrial Estate, Tralee.

for Wilma, Davin and Finn

Acknowledgements are due to the editors of the following where some of these poems, or versions of them, have been published:

The Anglo Celt; Ballyhaise Framed Book, 2007 (Cavan Co. Council); Cavan Anthology 2000 (Ed. Rita Kelly); Force 10 – issue 13 (Ed. Dermot Healy); The Living Streets – an anthology of the Ranelagh Arts Festival (Ed. Charles Crockatt, 7 Towers, 2009); Real Imaginings – an anthology of writing from Kerry (Ed. Tommy Frank O'Connor, Doghouse, 2009); Rhyme and Resin – Poetry Ireland collaboration between poets and artists at the R.H.A.; The Sunday Tribune; Windows Publications – Authors and Artists (Eds. Noel Monahan, Heather Brett).

Some poems were broadcast on *The Eleventh Hour* and *The Poetry Programme* (RTE Radio One) and on Dublin South City Radio.

Thanks to Cavan County Council for a bursary towards a residency at the Tyrone Guthrie Centre at Annaghmakerrig in 2008 where a number of these poems were revised;

to Noel King for his patience and his inner ear;

to Seamus Cashman for his careful reading;

to Noel Monahan for his encouragement;

to Sue, Kim and Danielle for their help in typing the many drafts of these poems;

and to Pat Galvin, Anne-Marie Glasheen, Eileen Sheehan and Barbara Smith for their proof-reading.

Contents

Fountain Pen

I kiss her lips
when words
desert me

trickle of water
at the hazel man's feet
on the dry river bed

River Annalee

Morning opens its nostrils
on the river plain,
breathes a dry ice chorus
of cumulus, nimbly drifting

over water and river fields.
Nothing stirs,
every sleeping thing sleeping,
earth and sky straining
to be one.

Through wet grass I trace
a dewy path, down tree roots'
slithery steps, to the water's
last lap.

Truth lies in this riverbed
where stones are smoothed
by the water's flow
and boughs arch achingly low
to kiss the river run.

I take into my hands
all the water
that hands can hold.

Tale of the Race

Brought up
on the howl
of the wind,
made lonely by trees;

by the eyes of the bridge,
streaming.

One dry,
to take the overflow,
one blocked up,
storing wood for winter heat.

Into a V we stepped
as traffic passed,
and oxtering our way up
on cold stone, we watched the river
run either side of an island
to the tale of the race.

Our heads were white waters swirling
and such was the movement
that no one can say, for certain,
whether island or bridge
water or child
really moved.

Pike

Beyond the Mill Marsh,
the river takes a turn for the deep,
dark pike-swallowing deep;

pike looking up at us,
looking down on them.

Meniscus eyes
dead eyeing us,
thread razor teeth,
clench wide open.

Our people ate pike
long before we heard tell
of trout or salmon.

My father brought one home
on a stick-hook, just like
the tick our teachers made
in our copies in school.

They say around here
the likes of it was never seen before.
They say around here
the likes of it will never be seen again.

Still I can see his scarlet gills,
slime gulping for air,
desperately trying
to talk things down.

Yew

The centre of the yew tree
was hollow
from playing.

An opened space to
let the voices in –

resin rising, resonating
like wind inside a reed flute.

We were careful to keep
its outer branches strong,

like fingers,
in cupped hands,
sealed.

Sealed tight,
to hold in
the concealment.

Logging

Hadn't we everything then,
you and I,
either side of
a long-toothed saw?

    Pushing
    and
Pulling.

Pushing
    and
    Pulling.

Inching our way
deeper
into firewood.

Knotted wood
lay open
on our wooden horse,

a line of cuts with
none complete
kept the log intact.

Side-saddled,
I fed him
incisions through a V.

I left him
with a handsaw
to cut
the whole way through.

Corgarive

When you are going, leave
the mouth of the ford of the fish behind you,
follow the path of the foot of the foal
and at the place of the fox
dare to take a turn left for Corgarive.

Corgarbh,
sharp turn,
sharp bend for home,
sharp whine of the wind,
rough words on the air
that scathe and cut and wound.

Still the preacher walks the lake –
a curlew weeps,
and a corncrake insists
that being extinct
is truly a thing of the past.

We Headed for Home Together

The saddle, wide and leathery,
held the seat of his trousers,

the crossbar held my bony frame
and I shunted from one thigh to another
to keep my balance, ease the hurt.

I felt my head against his chest,
watched my sandaled feet,
his big shoes on the pedals,
rim, spoke and rubber.
The road ran by,

the One Tree Cross, the river,
the bridge, the straight
and the lean into the incline of the church bray
brought his big body up and down,

up and down. I heard him heave.
I heaved and bent in rhythm to ease his strain,
his pincer-grip on the handlebars,
my orbit in motion.

On to Austins,
(the villagers had their own way with intimacies,
that played down the indulgence, the intent)

in for *the one*, as they would say,
to quench the *drouth*.

Sunday Mass goers had forgotten the dinner,
match supporters in for the post-mortem.

The one wandered into many,
the *drouth*, the bread and wine,
down the drain.

Poker by the fire would rekindle the dying day.
Sweet Afton smouldering on stakes;
scattered on the table,
half-crowns brown with yellow nicotine.

Outside, I held the bike,
propped it against the window,
climbed its big frame,
sat in the saddle,
tiptoes tipping the pedals.

Smoke billowed out
the up and down sash window.
They fed me a silencing procession
of Pepsi and Perri crisps until
I could take no more.

When the night was drip-dried,
the *anyone that has homes to go to*
was announced.

They filed out in ones and twos,
each momentarily more certain
in their uncertain world.

We headed for home together.

I walked the bike at an angle
to keep it upright.

My father completed the circle
with his own dark tilt.

Holding

In the wings of a father's arms,
two little girls lie sleeping.

He is quiet too,
on the river bank, dozing.

His throne,
a rabbit-warren opening.

His staff, a fishing rod
resting on a twig.

The spool's unravelling
and the catch of his life

escaping him.

In the Living Room

Sometime after Easter
I sat at the doorway
between the sleeping
of my father
and my son

one coming
one going

between worlds
I waited

Intensive Care

Your low tide revealed
a cry beneath white porcelain skin,
a lament for left-luggage –
the felony of the unfulfilled.

Heave deep and breathe, Mother,
blow out blocked tubes
of ancestors past,
feel again and touch
and see and sing
so that I can see you once
again, as you once were.

In Search of a Signal

Who changed the feckin station? he would ask.
Will you get up and turn on the match, will you?
Once a week I try to tune in
And what do I get?

Silence would fall, limbo on airwaves,
interference becoming part of the transmission.

I don't know, I don't know, he would say.

The sounds would sing a capella,
as he tracked the highway
from Hilversum to Prague, Oslo to Paris.

Back and forth he would go, impatiently,
the meniscus tracker moving
but finding no match between us.

I don't know, I don't know, he would repeat.

But I did know, even back then.
I had been playing with the bands –
medium wave, long wave and
my father's very, very short wave.

I had changed the frequency forever –
pushed me and him beyond our station.

Many years later, on a bed wracked with pain,
I washed his tired feet,
massaged the dry rot out with oil.

We tuned in together
to a new wavelength.
The signal was strong, intense to be precise.
And now that his is gone,
I repeat to myself like a prayer:
I don't know, I don't know, I don't know.

Wind

There at the beginning
There at the end
With the last heave
And suck of air

The wind takes root
in every opening it can find,
lays waste to the aftertaste
of the day before.

Takes hold in the haybarn,
swirls, wrenches bolt from socket,
leaving galvanize to flap a dying rhythm
on a lone girder.

Pulls and fandangoes with tree tops,
forces starlings and rooks to lift
in shadowy cloaks and call
out their cries.

*   *   *

Cold wind on the sweat of his back,
cold wind on the horse's mane.
Whup ya go, ya boy ya.
Tether rope takes the slack.

It blows down furrows as they grub in lines,
dries hessian lines on their knees,
palm lines of clay on their hands,
cap peak down and on and on.

The wind traces every move they make,
moulds the hollow of the hand
where they lingered longer
with the obstinate weed – the stubborn yarrow.

Now it comes through
the harness-room door,
spits rain at the souvenir saddle
girth, trace and bit.

In from the fields they come,
their faces – a faded yellow photograph
in a frame, hanging
sideways on a nail.

And the wind blows it
gently,
idly
on and on.

Let the Wind In

My father's room was decorated
in brighter colours than he'd been used to,
old furniture, dusted down,
for last days.

Beside his bed,
false teeth –
redundant molars,
incisors lost cut.

Dried flowers
dried out.

Losec,
            Prepulsid,
                        Duphillac,
pharmaceutical gods
of the twisted and knotted gut.

Open the window
let the wind in –

messenger to another world
free him from four walls,

feed him a final exit line.

Windfall

On the night of the big wind
they brought him home.

I awoke next morning to find
my oak, my ash all rolled up in one;
hewn to the ground.

Your fall revealed
a different side –
underbelly, underside, undergrowth
an underworld of stones and clay,
flesh and bones of the earth.

Thick canopy of leaves
shade me.
Sturdy boughs
protect me.
Roots to the ground
earth me.
Snarl of twisted wood
along your trunk,
electrify me.

On a Park Bench with Davin

Arms around each other,
like moss and twig entwined,
overhead an aeroplane roars,
something breaks inside
as I know that
one day
he too
will take flight.

Flight

for Finn

He rushed headlong to
the fall of cherry blossoms;

unseasonal snow shower
in spring.

By the handful he threw
them to the wind

and traced the flight
of a single petal,

airborne,
to another world.

Requiem for the Father

*God, give voice to an inarticulate mumbler who
stumbled on a Hail Mary*

Amid turmoil, truce and treaty
his breath came in in 1921,
lasted almost seventy-seven years,
one for every martyr
he would say.

Travelled the homeland –
Keelagh, Dresdernagh, Ardamagh,
Cearnóg, Drumcrow,
Drumaraw,

life and death
in a handful of townlands,
no need to go further.

He supported a wife
as best he could,
reared six children
ploughed fields, harrowed,
fenced the boundaries of the plot.

*Metal of crow bar
wood of the stake
tooth of the harrow
disc of the plough*

pray for us
as we break open the earth
together.

*   *   *

In a stable
teeming with knowledge
he tended horses,
wild, wild horses,
even spoke to them in his sleep.

Speak to them now Dad in your sleep
that they may carry you;

your activity tamed
by the umbilical cord
that grew inside you.

Amniotic fluid
to ferry you back to your maker.

Your river Styx,
no Charon to carry you,
but six strong children.

Your passage paid for
well in advance.

Grave diggers came –
not grave, oh no,
but full of laughter, mischief
and wickedness
like yourself.

They knew your kind
as they picked
and shovelled the earth.

And in the distance two wise men
headed for Shantemon,
in the direction of the past

to gather moss
with the fingers of Finn,
to soften your resting place.

They too, like you,
knew the comfort
of snow on Good Friday
to break your fall.

Casket of Oak
acorn of the past
burrow deeply into the
unyielding earth
and bring him
on your Ariel roots
upwards to the sky

At the palace of the King
tell them your stories,
your wondrous ballads
of Boru, O'Neill, and Dwyer.
Tell them your name – John Conaty (J.C.)
initialled well by your maker,
a good man, fit to carry a cross.

Your breath, our breath
came in, in '21,
left on a Sabbath in '98
of trouble, truce and treaty.

Mooring

The mooring rope is untied,
the vessel is put to sea

dead flat calm,

only line breaks
mark the wake,

silent winds blow,
their undertow ripping
at my sail.

Hearing Things

i

Temporally unsound,
and from time to time
hearing things,
I lie somewhere
between silence
and a word.

ii

Powdered rust and
wood-rot fall to ground,
I place a pen between
door and jamb, leave it to
write the hum
of all things unhinged.

iii

I go out on blustery nights
secure in the knowledge that
all are indoors.

Hard shoulders give
way to fallen boughs.

Field-gates fly skyward, opening
pastures of the moon.

Epitaphs litter words
in graveyards that plot
the arrival of
the next internee.

Hopelessly a last leaf clings
and I take shelter in a tomb
from a full force gale.

The Furrow of Memory

Lately, I have come to know
the coldness of stone;
barefoot, on a summer's morning

and the blackness
of the raven's wings,
snouting deep
in the furrow of memory

and the warmth of a baby's
head against my cheek,
when autumn colours turn.

I watch and a feather falls
from a nest,

warm air
clouding the window pane

I wipe away to see.

Half-Doors

Half-doors lie open,
half-light spills in.

Watches, clocks,
all timepieces
tick,

synchronised
to half-time.

*Half of the time we're gone
but we don't know where.**

Singing songs,

diminuendo,

on the lyre's

half-played melody.

* lines from Simon & Garfunkel, *The Only Living Boy in New York.*

Pigging

My mother reared pigs by hand,
big Landrace pigs, under
the colour, heat and light
of an infrared bulb.

Metal crate,
big sow on her side,
tits falling to the ground,
heavy with milk.

Nudging, climbing one over
the other, butting and voraciously
chomping, leaky milk, side
snouting onto straw.

Brushes of bristle
on bony backs,
opening and rising
feed after feed.

Swim

for Jane McCormick

listen .... shh ... she's coming ....

Each day she goes to the lake to swim,
she goes to take the waters in,
out in the lake, waist-high,
she severs her image from the sky.
Plunges down, then up,
drinks her reflection by the cup
of her hands.

She takes everything in,
not a single drop falls through.

listen .... shh ... she's coming ....

Muffled metronome.

A silent slipper-beat
to the lake.

Regular as day.

Regular as night.

The slipper-woman swims at night,
imperceptible, out of sight.
At midnight, disciples are few,
save the raven, pike,
curved-beak curlew,
ghost sallies,
birch of ashen bark,
opening the shore road in the dark.

Only a shadow of herself
takes up the walk by day.

The lake has its own tide,
slipper-moon tug of the sleeve
to the shore.

Silence of the slipper-moon,
silence again tomorrow,
treading to the lakeside,
little time left to borrow.

The slipper-woman makes no sound,
there's silence in her wake,
for God's sake, say nothing
when you see her walk upon the lake.

listen .... shh ... she's coming ....

Cat-like she may be,
soft slippering her way around
but nine lives are not that many
and she's counting down,
counting down,
measuring the hairline crack
on this merry-go-round.

Two swans, overhead,
their wings beat a fading rhythm,
feather white arc-waves,
sleep froth-lines,
sinking by the shore.

listen .... shh ... she's coming ....

Soggy bottoms to the lake,
paling posts and fence losing their
meaning to the flood.
Barbed wire, blunt from the water's edge.

Everything is mist and she is mist itself.
Slipper-soft catkin, heavy with rain,
willowing her way,
carrying the pilgrim's pain.

In her hand a knotted prayer.

So, leave yourself to grass and lichen
on the shore,
count cuckoo-spit like rosary beads,
pray in homage
for the moist touch of nature's lips,
sing the song of sallies on the shore,
let their shadow pencil lines write
the melody of all things unhinged.

Woman of the lake,

melancholy wind, lapping water to her feet.

I
    walk
    your
    curve
of
    sand
    and
    stone,

wait for your opening line,
a ripple word, billowing
across the lake,
inviting me in.

Lift your veil,
you've hidden your face too long.
In your ponderous sleep
rest easy, ruffled virgin,
rest deep.

I break your meniscus sheath,
free-fall,
plummet to the heights below,
down....down....
            and deeper down....
                down to the place,
                    where all rising comes from.

listen .... shh ... she's coming ....

When whales sing their songs

they sing them to the deep,

whale-music, high-pitched,
on a bass clef ocean floor,

a deep breathing,
slow-release kind of music,
like love
that is slow in the making;
bread rising,
a wash of sea to the shore.

Mission Sunday

Wind, homing pigeon of the sky,
you brought us Sahara dust
on a Sabbath morning.

It clung to windows, doors, rooftops,
covered our houses with your seal.

Mass goers,
intent on their weekly sacrifice,
wiped you clean.

Holy water,
Third World dirt removed.

They felt they could see again.

Swimmer

for Anne Marie

I. Solo

I could talk
to the walls, I suppose,
to the sink,
or the taps, maybe,
run it by them
hot or cold.

Against the window-pane
I could whisper it,
watch 'til my breath condenses
in droplets and necklace their
way groundwards.

No one around
to hear my broken words;
no one to hear
the heaving chokefuls
herald another let down,
another broken promise.

It's not the despair
that gets you.
No, it's the hope
that hurts.

Yes, it's the hope
that really hurts.

II. Relay

But hope you say
it must be
against hope and hurt;
the flowing tide,
the favourable current,
the thermal from a distant shore.
Clutch you say at every straw or cliché
of hope you can find.

Look back in your wake
at the tracks you make
in that sea,
and know that you open
a path for another to follow.

On dry land,
hold your breath,
listen.

Cargo

i

So many clothes
you wear
this winter.
I cannot feel
your body-heat
under so many layers.

ii

We live in separate rooms now,
you on your side of the wall,
me on mine,
both measuring distance.

The walls are thin.
I hear you breathe.
Out and in,
out then in.

iii

From another floor
you turn on your radio.
I turn on mine.
Music rises,
begins to swell,
stereophonic, in the stairwell.

iv

Subcutaneous –
I am a thin layer under your skin
and you are a thin layer under mine,
that all the exfoliation and deep cleansing
will not remove.

The cargo, though divided, lies
in the hold of two separate ships now.
Log book open,
destination written
on high seas.

So many ruins

to find in this place.
I chance upon them in the undergrowth
when I follow the river downstream.
Stones ensnared by grass,
I unravel their plight by hand.

The mossy shell,
the missing mortar,
the held and the withheld
that hold the foundations to the ground.

Pathways between these houses must be found.

Convolvulus grows around the hearths
sucking fire-milk words
from chimney breasts.

Bearings

for Paddy Sexton

i

Searchlights dim the pointers,
the North Star fades in the sky,
he reads the signs
for us to travel by.

Swallows check in with their flight plans
and swifts sleep on the wing,
when he sends word of prevailing
winds to carry them.

From his position in the tower, he scans
for signals, takes soundings, sightings,
sifts for turbulence,
and for calm:

speaks in hectopascals
of high and low pressure,
coming in off the Atlantic.
His words,

first words in the pilot's ear before landing,
last words, before departure –
air corridors, runways,
earthing the sky.

When I walk with him on the island
he is easy and steady
and in his wake,
on a path by *Trá Gheal*

I, too, begin to read the contours
of the land, the peaks and depressions,
my eye drawn to a headland
or an inlet, a gable end

or a gatepost, something in the distance,
something to come home by,
in case of heavy
weather.

Once he read the heavy weather
on my face, his hand,
a warm front on my shoulder,
to comfort me.

ii

But like you and me,
and the North Star, he too,
will lose light
and dim and fade,

a whispering wind,
faded out, like radio signals
fading out
at closedown.

Yet I hear him still
like shipping news
to vessels at sea;

hear him on winds,
From Carnsore Point to the Mizen,
Loop Head to Erris,
Rossan to Carlingford Lough,

dead calm, imminent,
dead calm, now

not a breath, not a sound,
on all coastal waters
and on the Irish Sea.

Altitude Sickness

I have summits of my own to climb,
ascents, new faces,
to be picked and chiselled.
Crampon tightropes tightening.
Holding ground on a thin wire.

There are no Sherpas left to guide me,
only the faint fragrance of a trail
hanging in the air.
And before despair
I take my head out of clouds –

Plunge –

Break ice-glass water on the lake, swim
to cool down from summery sun,
out past toe-gulch mud and algae,
past reed-ripples shorebound,
out to where, once, I saw the depths below –

Pike-pitch darkness –

I climb down again,
altitude sickness,
swimming in my brain.

Offering

The furniture had stood its ground
long enough.

Late one night
when all was quiet
it offered itself up
for removal.

out of the early morning mist

of a sudden
unannounced
like the spoor
of a hare
on dew

on a morning
when possibilities
seem pure
and something
is calling

Suspended

on a lip
of liminal land,

a spider unravelling
a thread,

adhesive holding
the line.

The web that takes
our breath away,

holds the air
we breathe.

The intricate spaces
catch a cold spell.

Wind tightens
its grip.

Ice blurs
the window pane.

I pay the price for altitude

and one look at the Sherpa's face
tells me the climb is done.

Breaker's Yard

Two wooden beams
for a workbench, a slick of oil
seeping through the grain.

A vice, mouth wide open,
with word of better parts to come.
A calendar stuck on March,

thumb-stained from leafing
and an invoice book, pink and white
alternate pages, undisturbed.

A phone line with no connection – receiver
dislodged, earpiece listening.

And the mouthpiece
talking to itself,
with no one around.

Everything wrenched apart in the yard,
standing in disconcerted piles,
each with its own.

Fagan's Yard kept us all on the road,
an organ cardholder, for travellers
with too many miles up.

Unapproved Road

Measured by the intervals
in the persistent barking
of a stray dog
at night

and the almost inaudible sound
of the occasional car
dissolving
into distance,

we wait on the open road,
listening for any word
that may come our way

Finding an Opening

Like fabric unravelling, 'til
the last thread is picked

down to the knot of the first tie.

The eye of a needle,
pincer fingers,

spittle and daub
pointing the way and,

chances are, the thread
will splinter many times

before it finds the opening.

Where are the Mourners

Now that this day has come.

When all is said and done,
it's down to the arc
of an opening
and closing door,

the passage through,
the dare-not-look-back
moment –
of going.

The latch,
click-clacking behind,
and the unmistakable sound
of   shut.

Flagstone of granite,
two steps,
down a path and
out a black, garden gate.

An electric saw whines
its way through timber,
on a building site
nearby

and somewhere,
autumn grass is surrendering
to the lawnmower's blade.

Wintering

The wind is coming
from a different direction now –
stops the river flowing;
bids the waterfall stand still.

In flight, the geese
undo their V,
and even the night owl
cannot see.

The arched and stiffened whitethorn
straightening, taking in air from
a different course;
its source, a mouth-opening place
between here and there,
now and then.

Parchment of white scrolls back
on the stricken birch,
inviting us to read
the manuscript beneath.

Chain

So how come
no one told me
where my father's bike went.

I suppose it went the way of the rest,
left in some outhouse

when the legs lost the power
to pedal, or someone said
that the roads weren't safe anymore.

Left to lie against a brown, leaky wall,
where galvanize never matched up
to the slate.

Slow drip, trickle and rust,

Never-ending chain
knotted on itself; twisting
with the will to move once more.

Lodgers
for Kathy Prendergast

Even the dust settles
in this grey
before dawn,

soothsayer eyes
say lightness
to everything living

and everything
dying,
and the dead.

Guests –
newcomers
and the pre-booked

in this boarding house of ours.

Grace

Her feet hold the earth firmly
her body, a rotating prism of light,

kanga billows the black contours of her thighs
nose, cheekbones chin ...

All comers hopelessly drawn in
to the arc of her hand when

she speaks against the blue sky
leaving notes for the birds to sing,

and the opening of her mouth as
she points to where she came from

spills all the co-ordinates I'll ever need.
North – cold stars to move by

South – so seeds may grow
West – to fade in and out on

and East, oh beautiful east –
the call to start again and again

and again, searching for a place
in between, where kanga billows
the black contours ...

Gathering Light

The Epiphany was yesterday,
and today is today.

Three windows look to the South.
A January sun hangs low in the sky,

shines through a rack of bones, a tree
in the distance.

This afternoon and its afternoon sleep
awakens in me the grey of watery light.

The epiphany was yesterday,
today is the day.

Flute Player

for Ciaran Carson

With a fine reed,
he lifted a G note

From deep down at the bottom
of the bog pool.

Spat out the suck and squelch of
muddy brown,

Rolled it out in his mouth and let it move
to a sound place.

Cast it high on the pitch of the roof,
sensed its pull under tongue-tide

And on steady breath and foot tap
he released his air to
an exaltation of starlings.

Tom Conaty, born 1957, is a teacher from Ballyhaise, Co. Cavan, now living in Dublin. He has two sons, Davin and Finn.

Poetry in Education and in collaboration with other artists is central to his work. He has created poetry, fiction, drama and film with, and for, children. He is a member of the Board of Directors, Poetry Ireland / Éigse Éireann and has acted as Consultant to the Arts Council in Arts Education, Programming and Policy.

Also available from DOGHOUSE:

Heart of Kerry – an anthology of writing

from performers at Poet's Corner, Harty's Bar, Tralee 1992-2003

Song of the Midnight Fox – Eileen Sheehan

Loose Head & Other Stories – Tommy Frank O'Connor

Both Sides Now - Peter Keane

Shadows Bloom / Scáthanna Faoi Bhláth – haiku by John W. Sexton,

translations, Gabriel Rosenstock

FINGERPRINTS (On Canvas) – Karen O'Connor

Vortex – John W. Sexton

Apples In Winter – Liam Aungier

The Waiting Room – Margaret Galvin

I Met A Man... Gabriel Rosenstock

The DOGHOUSE book of Ballad Poems

The Moon's Daughter – Marion Moynihan

Whales Off The Coast Of My Bed – Margaret O'Shea

PULSE – Writings on Sliabh Luachra – Tommy Frank O'Connor

A Bone In My Throat – Catherine Ann Cullen

Morning At Mount Ring – Anatoly Kudryavitsky

Lifetimes – Folklore from Kerry

Kairos – Barbara Smith

Planting a Mouth – Hugh O'Donnell

Down the Sunlit Hall – Eileen Sheehan

New Room Windows – Gréagóir Ó Dúill

pto

Slipping Letters Beneath the Sea – Joseph Horgan

Canals of Memory – Áine Moynihan

Arthur O'Leary & Arthur Sullivan – Musical Journeys from Kerry to the

Heart of Victorian England - Bob Fitzsimons

Crossroads – Folklore from Kerry

Real Imaginings – a Kerry anthology, edited by Tommy Frank O'Connor

Touching Stones – Liam Ryan

Where the Music Comes From – Pat Galvin

No Place Like It – Hugh O'Connell

The Moon Canoe – Jerome Kiely

Every DOGHOUSE book costs € 12, postage free, to anywhere in the world (& other known planets). Cheques, Postal Orders (or any legal method) payable to DOGHOUSE, also PAYPAL (www.paypal.com) to doghousepaypal@eircom.net

"Buy a full set of DOGHOUSE books, in time they will be collectors' items" - Gabriel Fitzmaurice, April 12, 2005.
DOGHOUSE
P.O. Box 312
Tralee G.P.O.
Tralee
Co. Kerry
Ireland
tel + 353 6671 37547
email doghouse312@eircom.net
www.doghousebooks.ie